Leukemia

By Judith Peacock

Consultant:
Barbara Asselin, MD
University of Rochester School of Medicine
Department of Pediatrics

Perspectives on Disease and Illness

LifeMatters
an imprint of Capstone Press
Mankato, Minnesota

LifeMatters books are published by Capstone Press
818 North Willow Street • Mankato, Minnesota 56001
http://www.capstone-press.com

Printed in the United States of America

Library of Congress Cataloging-in-Publication Data
Peacock, Judith, 1942–
      Leukemia / by Judith Peacock.
          p.   cm. — (Perspectives on disease and illness)
      Includes bibliographical references and index.
      Summary: Discusses the disease, its diagnosis and treatments, and
      related research.
      ISBN 0-7368-0282-7. — ISBN 0-7368-0294-0 (series)
      1. Leukemia Juvenile literature. [1. Leukemia. 2. Diseases.]
      I. Title. II. Series.
      RC 643.P38 2000
      616.99′419—dc21   99-15709
                                                CIP

Staff Credits
Kristin Thoennes, Rebecca Aldridge, editors; Adam Lazar, designer; Kim Danger, photo researcher

Photo Credits
Cover: The Stock Market/©Howard Sochurek, bottom; PNI/©Digital Vision, left, right; PNI/©RubberBall, middle
Index Stock Photography, Inc./20; ©John Riley, 38
Photo Network/©Jeff Greenberg, 50
©James L. Shaffer, 59
Unicorn Stock Photos/©MacDonald, 28, 57; ©Les Van, 8; ©Tom, DeAnn McCarthy, 15; ©Tom
McCarthy, 42; ©Karen Holsinger Mullen, 44
Uniphoto Picture Agency/©Rick Brady, 33
Visuals Unlimited/6, 23, 31; ©John Forsythe, 17; ©John D. Cunningham, 24; ©Mark Gibson, 48; ©Jeff
Greenberg, 49

A 0 9 8 7 6 5 4 3 2 1

Table of Contents

Chapter Overview

Leukemia is cancer of the blood. The body produces a large number of abnormal white blood cells. Leukemia disrupts the production of normal blood cells.

A person with leukemia may bruise easily. Leukemia lowers a person's ability to fight infection.

The cause of leukemia is not known. Researchers have identified several risk factors. These include exposure to high-energy radiation and certain chemicals. Certain genetic disorders also have been linked to leukemia.

Leukemia can be a deadly disease.

Chapter 1

What Is Leukemia?

"You have leukemia, Sarah." The doctor's words stunned Sarah. She **Sarah, Age 16** looked at her parents. Her mother's eyes were full of tears. Her father seemed pale and shaken.

Leukemia. Leukemia. Leukemia. The word echoed in Sarah's head. Leukemia. That means cancer, she thought to herself. A feeling of dread filled her body. Sarah looked at the doctor. "Am I going to die?" she asked.

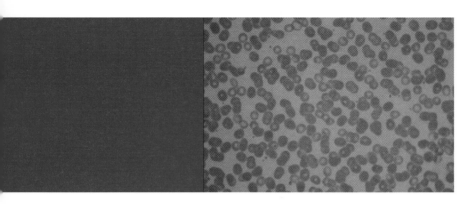

The doctor's diagnosis terrified Sarah and her parents. Leukemia can be a deadly disease. In the United States, leukemia kills more children between the ages of 2 and 15 than any other disease. Each year, leukemia develops in about 4 in every 100,000 youngsters.

Leukemia is not just a disease that children get. In fact, it strikes 10 times as many adults as children. More than half of all leukemia cases occur in persons over age 60.

Cancer of the Blood

Leukemia is a type of cancer. There are over 100 different types of cancer. All cancers have one thing in common. Abnormal body cells divide, multiply out of control, and then spread. In leukemia, the blood cells do that.

Knowing about normal blood cells helps to understand leukemia. The blood consists of a fluid called plasma and three types of cells: white blood cells, red blood cells, and platelets. White blood cells fight infection. They destroy bacteria and viruses that invade the body. Red blood cells carry oxygen from the lungs to all parts of the body. They give blood its red color. Platelets help form blood clots. Clots control bleeding when a person gets injured.

Most blood cells are formed in bone marrow. The marrow is the soft, spongy center of bones. Under normal circumstances, the white blood cells circulate, or travel, to the lymph nodes, the liver, and the spleen. The cells stay there until they are needed.

A healthy body produces blood cells in an orderly, controlled way. In leukemia, the marrow produces a large number of abnormal white blood cells. These cells are immature, or young. They look different. They do not function properly.

Effects of Leukemia

Leukemia affects a person in several ways. The person may become anemic. This means that when leukemia cells flood the marrow, they crowd out the red blood cells. The blood looks thin, which makes the person look pale. He or she becomes weak and tired because thin blood cannot carry enough oxygen to body tissues.

The number of platelets also drops. This decreases the blood's clotting ability. A person bruises easily. He or she may bleed excessively from a cut or a nosebleed.

Leukemia cells lack the ability to fight infections. The person is more likely to pick up colds and the flu. As the leukemia gets worse, the person has no immunity, or protection, against serious illnesses.

Finally, the person's lymph nodes, spleen, liver, and kidneys swell. This is because of the high number of abnormal white blood cells that are circulating there. The cells overpopulate those areas of the body, causing them to swell.

Causes of Leukemia

Sarah Wonders Why

Sarah wondered what she had done to cause her leukemia. She didn't smoke or drink. She didn't do drugs. Sarah thought she was a good person. Was she being punished for something she had done?

The worst nuclear accident in history occurred at the Chernobyl Nuclear Power Plant in 1986. An explosion sent tons of radioactive material over northern Ukraine and other parts of Europe. Researchers continue to study the disaster's impact on the health of people living in the area. In particular, researchers are looking for cases of cancer, including leukemia.

A person's behavior can lead to some types of cancer. For example, smoking can cause lung cancer. Too much sunbathing can lead to skin cancer. This is not the case with leukemia in children and teens. Children and teens with leukemia did not do anything to cause their cancer. They are not being punished.

Medical researchers believe that a change in a person's genes leads to cancer. Genes are the materials in cells that determine traits such as eye color or hair color. Researchers are looking into why normal genes change into cancer genes. Most often, the cause of a person's leukemia is not known. However, researchers have identified several factors that put people at risk for getting the disease.

Exposure to Large Amounts of High-Energy Radiation
Studies show that people living near an atomic bomb blast get leukemia at a higher rate than normal. An accident at a nuclear power plant also could release high-energy radiation into the environment. Some studies suggest a possible link between exposure to low-energy radiation and leukemia. Power lines and electric appliances release this type of radiation. More research is needed to prove this link.

X rays are a form of radiation. Remember the last time you had X rays at the dentist? The dentist protected your body with a lead shield. He or she stepped out of the room when the X rays were being taken. These measures protect both you and the dentist.

Certain Birth Defects or Genetic Disorders

One genetic disorder is Down syndrome. People with Down syndrome have an extra chromosome. Children born with this condition are more likely to have leukemia.

Exposure to High Levels of Certain Chemicals

One dangerous chemical is benzene. It is used in the manufacture of medicines, dyes, and many other products. Workers who breathe benzene vapors have a high rate of leukemia.

Viruses

Researchers have linked viruses to certain leukemias in animals. More research is needed to understand this link.

Researchers continue to study risk factors for leukemia. They do know that leukemia is not contagious. It is not spread from person to person like the flu or a cold. It is safe to be near people with leukemia.

Points to Consider

What do you think when you hear the word *cancer?*

How much do you know about cancer? How much did you know about leukemia before you read this chapter?

Have any of your family members had cancer? What is the disease like for them? What was it like for the rest of the family?

Chapter Overview

Leukemia can be acute or chronic. Acute leukemia gets worse rapidly. The number of abnormal white cells multiplies quickly. Chronic leukemia develops more slowly. The body can function because it continues to produce enough normal blood cells.

There are four main types of leukemia: acute lymphocytic leukemia, acute myelogenous leukemia, chronic lymphocytic leukemia, and chronic myelogenous leukemia.

Acute lymphocytic leukemia, or ALL, is the most common type in children.

Chapter 2

Types of Leukemia

There are several types of leukemia. They are grouped in two ways: by how quickly the disease develops and by the type of cell affected.

How Quickly the Disease Develops

Leukemia can be acute or chronic. Signs of acute leukemia appear suddenly. The number of abnormal white cells develops quickly. The disease rapidly gets worse.

Rudolf Virchow, a German biologist, discovered leukemia in 1845. While performing an autopsy, he noticed a high number of white blood cells in the dead person's bloodstream. For this condition, Virchow suggested the Greek name *leukemia,* which means "white blood." He later was the first to describe the two major types of leukemia.

One evening, Stan sat at his desk at home. He had to finish writing a paper for English. Stan suddenly slumped over his computer. He complained of head and neck pain. His vision was blurred. His family brought him to the hospital emergency room. Within four days, he was diagnosed with acute leukemia. Stan began fighting for his life.

Stan, Age 15

Chronic leukemia develops more slowly. It gets worse gradually. The person's body continues to produce enough healthy blood cells. The person may be able to live a normal life for several years.

Howie Wilson's mother was diagnosed with chronic leukemia four years ago. **Howie, Age 12** Medications help control her symptoms. Mrs. Wilson works full-time in an office. She is president of her women's group. She enjoys doing things with her family. Howie knows that one day his mother may become very sick.

Type of Cell Affected

There are two main types of white blood cells: lymphocytes and granulocytes. Leukemia involving lymphocytes is called lymphocytic leukemia. Leukemia involving granulocytes is called myeloid or myelogenous leukemia.

Each year in the United States, there are about 1,300 new cases of acute lymphocytic leukemia in children.

Combined Description

The two ways of grouping leukemia are usually combined. This results in four main types.

Acute Lymphocytic Leukemia (ALL)

This is the most common type in children. ALL is sometimes called childhood leukemia. ALL usually strikes between the ages of two and eight. More boys than girls get it. ALL also affects adults, especially adults age 65 and older.

Acute Myelogenous Leukemia (AML)

Both children and adults get this type. AML also is called acute nonlymphocytic leukemia, or ANLL. This is the most common type of leukemia seen in adults.

Chronic Lymphocytic Leukemia (CLL)

This type of leukemia affects adults age 55 and older. CLL never appears in children.

Chronic Myelogenous Leukemia (CML)

This type mainly affects adults. A small number of children may get CML.

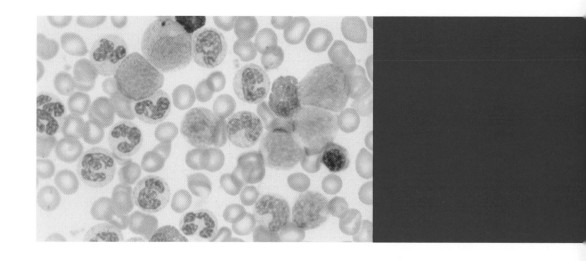

Points to Consider

How might a diagnosis of acute leukemia change a person's life?

How might a diagnosis affect a person's family?

In what way is chronic leukemia like a time bomb?

Chapter Overview

Early diagnosis of leukemia is important. The sooner treatment begins, the greater the chance of curing or controlling the disease.

Common symptoms of leukemia include anemia, fever, bleeding, bruising, pain in joints and bones, and persistent infections. Leukemia resembles other illnesses in its early stages. This makes it difficult to diagnose.

Diagnosing leukemia begins with the person's medical history, a general examination, and a description of symptoms. Blood tests help reveal the presence of leukemia. Bone marrow tests, X rays, and spinal taps confirm the diagnosis.

Most doctors agree that children and teens should know the truth about their leukemia.

Chapter 3

Diagnosing Leukemia

Early diagnosis, or determination, of leukemia is very important. This is especially true in the case of acute leukemia. People with acute leukemia need treatment right away. Without treatment, they may have only a few months to live.

Symptoms of Leukemia

A diagnosis of leukemia usually comes about in one of two ways. People with acute leukemia feel sick. They may notice something unusual about their body. They go to the doctor to find out the cause of their symptoms.

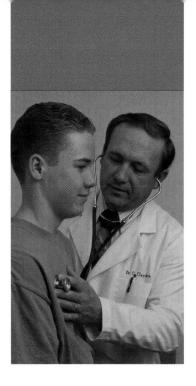

People with chronic leukemia may have no obvious signs for a long time. They may have only mild symptoms. They might go to the doctor for a routine checkup. The doctor then discovers the leukemia during the examination.

Toby, Age 14

One day, Toby was teasing his little brother. Toby's brother threw a small rubber ball at him. It hit Toby's face. Toby's cheek turned purplish-red almost right away. The boys' parents saw the bruise. "This isn't normal," they both thought. "A ball that lightweight shouldn't cause a bruise like this."

Toby's parents began to worry. Maybe something was wrong with Toby. He did seem tired all the time, and he was losing weight. Toby's mother made an appointment for Toby to see a doctor at the clinic.

Fast Fact

Toby showed symptoms of leukemia. Common symptoms of leukemia include the following:

Weakness and fatigue

Loss of appetite or weight

Bruising easily and bleeding without clotting

Frequent infections

Pale complexion, or skin

Fever, chills

Tiny red spots under the skin

Pain in joints and bones

Like all blood cells, leukemia cells travel throughout the body. Leukemia symptoms depend on the number of abnormal white cells and where they collect in the body. In acute leukemia, the abnormal cells may collect in the brain or spinal cord. The person may have headaches, vomiting, confusion, loss of muscle control, and seizures. In chronic leukemia, the abnormal cells may gradually collect in various parts of the body. The person may have stomach, kidney, and skin problems.

Here are the seven warning signs for cancer. If you experience one, check with your doctor. Don't wait.

1. Change in bowel or bladder habits
2. A sore that does not heal
3. Unusual bleeding or discharge
4. Thickening or lump in breast or elsewhere
5. Indigestion or difficulty swallowing
6. Obvious change in a wart or mole
7. Nagging cough or hoarseness

Difficulties in Diagnosis

Diagnosing leukemia can be difficult. In its early stages, leukemia resembles other illnesses. Toby's parents thought that Toby had a bad case of the flu or had low iron. Toby was run down, and his white blood cell count was high. The doctor at the clinic diagnosed mononucleosis.

When joint pain developed, the doctor thought Toby might have juvenile arthritis. Toby's symptoms got worse. Finally, the doctor referred Toby to an oncologist. An oncologist is a doctor who specializes in diagnosing and treating cancer.

Steps in Diagnosis

Diagnosing leukemia involves several steps. Doctors first take the person's medical history. They want to know about the person's health in the past. They also want to know about serious illnesses among family members. This information might help to explain the person's symptoms.

The next step is a physical exam. Doctors observe the person's general health. They check blood pressure, temperature, and heart rate. In addition, they check for swelling in the liver, spleen, and lymph nodes. Doctors listen carefully as the person describes his or her symptoms.

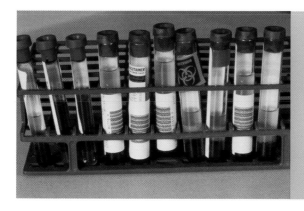

Blood tests are an important step in diagnosing leukemia. Laboratory technicians place a sample of the person's blood under a microscope. They can tell if leukemia cells are present. They also may be able to tell the type of leukemia. Chemical tests of the blood tell more about the disease.

If leukemia is suspected, doctors will remove cells from the person's bone marrow and examine them. A bone marrow test can confirm the diagnosis. It also can reveal the type of leukemia. Knowing the type is important for planning treatment. Some people like to get a second doctor's opinion before beginning treatment.

Toby's Test

Toby lay on his stomach on an examining table. The technician placed a pillow beneath his hips. She numbed Toby's hip with an anesthetic. Then she inserted a long, hollow needle into Toby's hipbone. The technician withdrew a small amount of liquid bone marrow. "Yeowwwwww!" Toby cried. "That really hurts!" After about 15 minutes, the procedure was finally over.

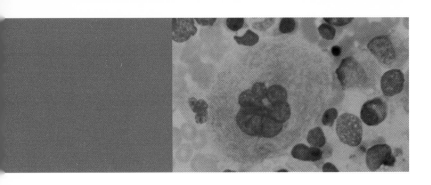

Toby had a bone marrow aspiration. A bone marrow biopsy uses a larger needle. Both procedures remove a small amount of bone or marrow.

The final step is to find out how far the leukemia has spread. For this, doctors use X rays and a spinal tap, or lumbar puncture. In a spinal tap, a doctor withdraws one or two teaspoons of spinal fluid from the spinal cord. The fluid can show whether the disease has spread to the brain and nervous system. Spinal taps and bone marrow exams also are done to check the progress of treatment. They can be very painful.

Learning the Truth

Toby's Diagnosis

Toby was diagnosed with acute lymphocytic leukemia. His parents were shocked. They didn't know what to say to him. Toby had already known that something was seriously wrong. All the tests and doctors' appointments told him that. Toby wanted to know the truth. "After all," he said, "it's my body. I'm the one who has to fight this thing. I want to know what I'm up against."

When children are diagnosed with leukemia, their parents may wonder what to tell them. Should they explain that the treatment will be long and painful? Should they acknowledge the seriousness of the disease? Parents may think the truth will be too frightening.

"My parents were never straight with me about my leukemia. When my dad bought me a mountain bike for no reason, I knew I was very sick."
—Chip, age 15

Most doctors believe that telling the truth is best. Children should be told that they have a serious illness but that it is treatable. They should be told in terms appropriate for their age level. Teens are capable of understanding their illness. They can understand the reasons for their symptoms.

Open and honest communication might relieve children and teens from fear of the unknown. It lets them know they are free to talk about their feelings. It encourages them to participate actively in their treatment.

Points to Consider

Have you ever had something wrong with you and you didn't know the reason? How did you feel?

What would you do if you found out you had leukemia?

Has anyone in your family ever been diagnosed with a serious illness? How did you react?

What should Toby's parents say to his six-year-old brother about Toby's leukemia?

Chapter Overview

Treatment for acute leukemia attempts to kill the growth of leukemia cells so they never grow back. Doctors consider a person cured if there are no symptoms for five years after treatment.

Chemotherapy and radiation therapy are the main treatments for leukemia. Doctors may try a bone marrow transplant for some people.

Treatments for leukemia may cause troublesome side effects such as hair loss, vomiting, and fatigue. Supportive therapy helps to relieve a person's discomfort.

Chapter 4

Treatment for Leukemia

Treatment for leukemia aims at complete remission. Remission means that the person no longer has signs of leukemia. The person's symptoms may disappear and then return later. This is called a relapse. Most doctors say that a person is cured if he or she shows no symptoms for five years after treatment.

Treatment for leukemia is not simple because each person is different. Doctors design a treatment plan to fit each individual's needs. They consider the person's age, symptoms, and general health. They consider the type of leukemia, how far it has spread, and whether the person has had cancer before.

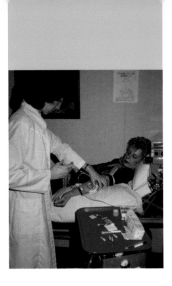

Chemotherapy

Chemotherapy is the most common way to treat leukemia. Chemotherapy means drug therapy. The person receives one or more powerful drugs. The drugs kill leukemia cells or slow their growth.

A program of chemotherapy varies from person to person. People receive different kinds and amounts of drugs. The drugs may be put right into the veins with an intravenous (IV) injection. The drugs also may be given in pill form or as a shot. People may receive chemotherapy in the hospital, at the doctor's office, or at home.

Stages of Chemotherapy

Chemotherapy usually is done in two main stages. During the first stage, the person receives intensive amounts of anticancer drugs. This stage continues until the person shows no signs of the leukemia. It may last from several weeks to several months.

During the second stage, the person continues to receive chemotherapy but in smaller doses. He or she can return to a more normal routine. The person has regular checkups, blood tests, and bone marrow exams or spinal taps to check for a relapse. This stage may last for two or three years or longer.

Children and teens with leukemia must endure constant needle pokes. They are poked for blood tests, IVs, bone marrow tests, and spinal taps. Some leukemia patients choose to have a catheter. The catheter is a flexible plastic tube that is used as a port. Surgeons implant it into a large vein in the upper chest. Medical staff do not have to find a new vein for each IV. Instead, they feed the drugs into the tube's top, which sticks out from the chest. After the treatment, they cap the tube and tape it in place.

Mary, Age 13

Mary is in her second round of chemotherapy. She stayed in the hospital for almost a month for the first round. Now she goes to the doctor's office once a week. She takes her chemo pills at home at night.

Mary's grandpa drives her to the doctor's office and then comes back for her. In the chemo room, Mary sits in a big, leather chair. Other people are there, too. Margie, the nurse, knows the least painful way to hook up and start Mary's IV bag. Mary reads a book or listens to tapes during her treatment. Sometimes she just closes her eyes and dozes while the drugs drip into her veins.

Mary is glad to be this far in her chemotherapy. She has been able to return to school and be with her friends. The only bad part is her hair—or lack of it. The chemotherapy has made her completely bald. Mary sometimes wears a wig. Most often, she wears a baseball cap or a brightly colored scarf. Mary's friends think her bald head is a badge of courage.

Did You Know?

Surgery usually is not a treatment for leukemia because leukemia is systemic. That means it runs throughout the entire body. There is no tumor, or growth, that can be cut out.

Side Effects of Chemotherapy

Chemotherapy can cause unpleasant side effects such as Mary's hair loss. Anticancer drugs go after any quickly dividing cell. The cells may or may not be leukemia cells. Cells in the hair, skin, mouth, stomach, and intestines normally divide quickly. Anticancer drugs kill these healthy cells, too. As a result, in addition to hair loss, the person may have an upset stomach after chemotherapy. He or she may feel tired and have mouth sores and dry skin.

Side effects from chemotherapy vary from person to person. People react differently to drugs. Not all drugs produce the same side effects.

Radiation Therapy

Doctors may use radiation for treatment of leukemia in the central nervous system and in the testicles. The radiation damages the leukemia cells or stops them from growing. Radiation therapy does not make the person radioactive.

Radiation is given in two ways. It may be given to the whole body or to only one area. The person lies on a table. High-energy rays come from a machine overhead. The procedure lasts for only a few minutes.

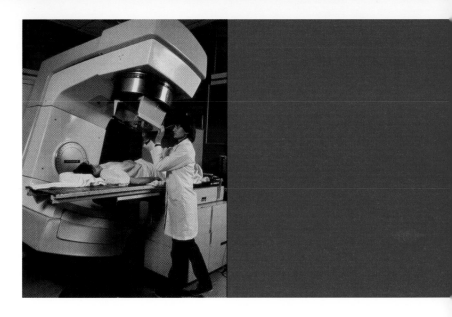

Radiation also causes side effects. The person may feel very tired for some time after the treatment. Nausea, vomiting, and loss of appetite are other side effects. If radiation is directed to the head, the person may have hair loss. The scalp and skin can become red, dry, itchy, and tender.

Some side effects of radiation therapy are long lasting. Children who receive radiation to the brain may have problems with learning and coordination. Boys who receive radiation to the testicles may not be able to have children later on. In these cases, doctors use radiation only if absolutely necessary. They give the lowest doses possible.

Bone Marrow Transplant

Doctors may try a bone marrow transplant for a seriously ill person. They destroy the person's leukemia-producing bone marrow with heavy doses of drugs and radiation. Then they inject healthy bone marrow into the person's bloodstream. They hope that the transplanted bone marrow will produce healthy white blood cells.

The National Marrow Donor Program (NMDP) began in 1987. It now has over three million potential donors. More volunteers are needed. The program especially needs more African-American, Hispanic, Asian/Pacific Islander, and Native American donors. A potential donor should be between the ages of 18 and 60 and in good health.

The healthy marrow usually comes from a donor. The donor's marrow must exactly match the person's marrow. The donor is often a member of the person's family. Relatives are more likely to have matching bone marrow. In some cases, the person's own marrow is used. The marrow is removed, treated to destroy leukemia cells, and then injected.

A bone marrow transplant can be dangerous. It is successful about 50 percent of the time. Side effects include an increased risk of infection and bleeding. The person also is at risk for graft-versus-host disease. This occurs when the new cells attack the person's cells. A battle between donor cells and host cells endangers the person's health.

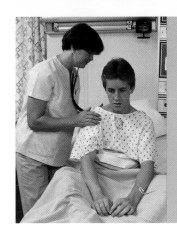

Alfonzo needed a bone marrow transplant to save his life. His family members had their blood tested. No one's tissue type matched Alfonzo's. A match could not be found among the family's friends either.

Alfonzo, Age 17

Alfonzo's doctors turned to the National Marrow Donor Program (NMDP). This database contains names of potential bone marrow donors. After a long search, only one possible match was found among thousands of names. The marrow belonged to a man living 800 miles away. He was still willing to be a donor.

On the day of Alfonzo's transplant, a medical cooler arrived at the hospital. Inside was a small bag of what looked like blood. It was bone marrow from the donor. The medical staff hooked up the bag to Alfonzo's IV. The bone marrow slowly dripped into his body.

After the transplant, Alfonzo struggled with rashes, uncontrolled bleeding, and pain. But the transplant was working. Tests showed that Alfonzo's body was producing healthy white blood cells. Alfonzo hoped one day to meet the man who had saved his life.

Supportive Therapy

Another kind of therapy is supportive therapy. Supportive therapy goes along with the other kinds of treatment. Its purpose is to prevent or control the side effects of chemotherapy and radiation. It also is meant to give the person a better quality of life.

Supportive therapy includes giving drugs to control nausea and vomiting. Doctors prescribe antibiotics to protect against infections. Supportive therapy also includes transfusions of red blood cells to help the person feel less tired. Transfusions of platelets help control bleeding.

All blood used for transfusions comes from volunteer donors. Less than 5 percent of the population donates blood. More people are needed to donate blood and to donate more often.

Points to Consider

How could you help a friend with leukemia during his or her treatment?

Do you know anyone who has been treated for cancer? What did the treatment plan involve?

What could you do to publicize the need for more bone marrow donors?

Do you know anyone who has donated blood or marrow? What was the experience like for that person?

Chapter Overview

People with leukemia and their families experience high levels of stress. The support of others can help people through their ordeal.

There are many sources of support for people with leukemia and their families. These include health care providers, mental health professionals, social workers, and organizations to assist people with cancer. Other people with cancer, cancer survivors, and friends and relatives also can provide support.

Support can take many forms. It can be information, financial aid, or counseling. It can be a willingness to listen and a shoulder to cry on. Practical acts such as running errands or watering houseplants also are forms of support.

Chapter 5

Finding Support

People with leukemia and their families experience high levels of stress. Taking care of a seriously ill family member can be exhausting. It is difficult to keep up with jobs and other responsibilities. There are many things to worry about, including the high cost of medical treatment. Most of all, everyone worries about the future. Fortunately, people and groups are available to lend support to those with leukemia and their families.

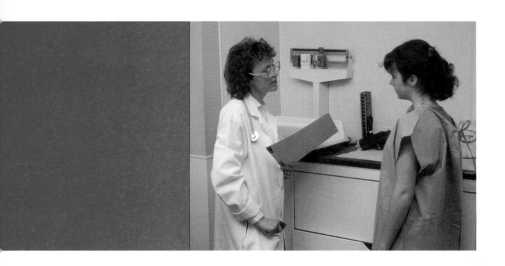

Health Care Providers

Many health care professionals are involved in caring for a person with leukemia. These professionals work as a team. Each contributes special knowledge and skills. Having a team of experts on hand can lessen a family's anxiety.

People with leukemia usually have several doctors. One of these doctors coordinates care. This doctor provides support by explaining treatment options and answering questions. People with leukemia should provide their doctor with accurate information. They should let their doctor know about their moods and physical well-being. This helps the doctor plan treatment. Open and honest conversations with the doctor can help reduce anxiety.

People with leukemia often must spend time in the hospital. As a result, they probably have more contact with nurses than any other health care provider. Nurses not only take care of physical needs, they also provide emotional support. They listen to people's worries and sympathize with what they are going through.

Many children and teens with leukemia must travel to hospitals in distant cities to obtain medical care. Ronald McDonald Houses provide their families with a low-cost place to stay near the hospital. McDonald's Restaurants opened the first Ronald McDonald House in Philadelphia in 1974. Since then, more than 100 have sprung up around the United States and overseas.

During treatment for leukemia, people may not feel like eating. Good nutrition, however, is important for getting better. Dietitians help people with leukemia eat well.

A stay in a hospital can be stressful. Patient-care coordinators can answer questions and resolve problems. They can help communicate a person's needs to the hospital staff. Discharge planners help arrange for the care of the person after he or she leaves the hospital.

Mental Health Professionals

A serious illness affects the emotions as well as the body. It is normal for people with leukemia to feel angry, sad, and frightened. Mental health counselors are available to help people and their families deal with these feelings. Psychologists and psychiatrists can help people who are severely depressed. Many people find comfort talking with spiritual leaders such as rabbis, priests, and ministers.

First Connection is a program of the Leukemia Society of America. It matches healthy cancer survivors with newly diagnosed people. The volunteer survivors visit or call the person. They offer an opportunity to talk with someone who has had the disease.

Social Workers

Social workers are available to assist with the many concerns, feelings, and questions related to leukemia. Social workers can assist the family in dealing with hospital policies and outside agencies. Social services are for the patient, family, friends, and even schools.

Social workers also are available for in-depth counseling. People have different emotional responses to a serious illness. The social worker can help with marriage problems or conflicts between parents and children.

Social workers also help with practical needs that patients and their families have. For example, social workers can give assistance with financial aid, transportation, and short-term housing. They can help find community resources.

Private Nonprofit Organizations

Several private nonprofit organizations exist to assist people with leukemia and their families. These organizations also support research on leukemia. They include the Leukemia Society of America (LSA), the American Cancer Society (ACS), and the Candlelighters Childhood Cancer Foundation (CCCF).

Here are some of the services these groups provide:

- Free information about leukemia and treatment methods

- Support groups for children and teens with leukemia, their parents, and their siblings

- Financial help or assistance finding sources of financial aid

- Referrals to cancer specialists

- Counseling

Government Services

The National Cancer Institute (NCI) is the federal government's main agency for cancer research. It also operates the Cancer Information Service (CIS). This is a nationwide telephone service. Specially trained staff members answer questions from callers and send out NCI materials. The phone number is 1-800-4-CANCER. Numbers that begin with 1-800 do not cost any money.

Other People With Cancer

Other people with cancer can be a source of emotional support. People with cancer often share a special bond. They know what having cancer is like. They can talk about things they may not want to talk about with their families. Many people with cancer have a bright outlook. They are determined to beat their illness. These people can be role models for others.

This is Dion's first time at Camp Baldy. Camp Baldy is for kids with cancer. Dion was diagnosed with leukemia one year ago.

Dion, Age 14

Camp Baldy is like other summer camps in many ways. The kids go swimming, boating, hiking, and horseback riding. There also are arts and crafts, singing around the campfire, and games.

Camp Baldy is different in some ways, too. For instance, at four o'clock every afternoon, the kids stop what they are doing and go to the med shed. There, a nurse dispenses their daily medications. The kids also have regular group sessions with their counselors. They talk about what it's like to have cancer.

Dion likes Camp Baldy. It's nice to be in a place where other people don't stare at his bald head. Several other kids are bald or fuzzy-headed, too. Dion doesn't have to explain why he sometimes feels tired or why he sometimes gets depressed. The other kids understand. They're going through the same thing.

The Internet is another place to meet cancer survivors. People with cancer and survivors, including teens with leukemia, have created their own web pages on the World Wide Web. They tell their experiences with cancer. They invite other people to contact them.

Cancer Survivors

The number of people who survive cancer continues to increase. These people provide a unique source of support. They can share information about treatment. They can tell people with cancer what to expect. Most of all, they give people and their families hope.

Dawn is a nurse on the oncology floor of a children's hospital. Dawn chose this job for **Dawn, Age 23** a reason. She wants to show her young patients and their families that it is possible to survive cancer. She is living proof.

Dawn was a cancer patient in this very same hospital. She was diagnosed with acute lymphocytic leukemia at age four. Dawn went through several years of chemotherapy and other painful treatment. By the time she was 10, her cancer was in remission. Dawn went on to have a normal adolescence.

When the time is right, Dawn tells her young patients and their families about her experience. Her story gives them hope. They see a survivor who is healthy and has a good life. Dawn helps them think about the future in a positive way.

Friends and Relatives

Friends and relatives can provide emotional and practical support. Emotional support may include visits, telephone calls, and cards. A hug or a pat on the shoulder lets people with leukemia know they are not alone. Practical support can take many forms. Friends and relatives might prepare a meal for the family, run errands, or provide transportation to doctors' appointments.

Most friends and relatives want to help. Sometimes they do not know what to do. Then people with leukemia and their families need to let their needs be known. Friends and relatives also may wonder what to say about the person's illness. People with leukemia and their families can take the lead here, too. They can say, "I do (or I don't) want to talk about it." It is usually best to be open and honest. This helps prevent fear and misunderstanding.

The Leukemia Society of America was founded in 1949 by two parents whose only son died of leukemia. They saw a need for a separate organization to improve the quality of life for people with leukemia and their families.

Points to Consider

What help would your family need if a family member became seriously ill? Whom could you count on?

How would your life change if a parent or sibling had to be in the hospital?

Come up with a list of practical things you could do to help a neighbor dealing with a medical crisis.

Chapter Overview

Living with leukemia can be especially hard for teenagers.

Leukemia can affect a teen's self-esteem, feelings of independence, and relationships with others. Teens with leukemia may have problems doing well in school.

Teens with leukemia may wonder if they will get well and stay well. They may worry about the future. It is important to know that childhood leukemia is one of the most treatable forms of cancer.

There are many ways teens with leukemia can cope with their illness.

Chapter 6

Living With Leukemia

Leukemia is hard to deal with at any age. It is especially hard for teenagers. Leukemia goes against many things teens are trying to achieve.

Body Image and Self-Esteem

An attractive physical appearance is important to most teens. They want to look their best. Leukemia can make it difficult to look good. Teens going through chemotherapy may have little or no hair. They may be underweight or overweight. Their faces may be puffy and red. They may appear tired and worn out.

Ellen's leukemia is in remission. Her hair has grown back. She is back to her normal weight. She looks happy and healthy. Ellen has almost forgotten how she looked during her chemotherapy. She is just glad to be healthy again. If she had to look terrible to get better, then it was worth it!

Ellen, Age 15

Becoming Independent

Most teens look forward to being on their own. They want to be able to do things for themselves. Leukemia makes teens dependent on their parents and doctors. Teens with leukemia may resent losing control of their life. They may rebel against their treatment. They may become angry with overprotective parents. Counseling can help teens understand their feelings.

During the first stages of treatment, teens with leukemia may feel very sick. They may be relieved to have someone caring for and comforting them. One teen says he would never have made it through treatment without his parents' help. Another teen says she and her mother grew closer during her illness.

Friendships

Friendships with others their age are important to most teens. They also may want to have a boyfriend or girlfriend. Leukemia makes it difficult to maintain friendships. Teens who miss a lot of school may have a hard time keeping in touch with friends. If they're back in school, they may be too tired to do things with friends. Teens with leukemia may not be able to go certain places with their friends. They might pick up colds and other infections in crowded restaurants and theaters.

Some teens may feel uncomfortable around a person with leukemia. They may not know what to say or do. They may avoid that person. Even friends who were once close may get tired of the person's illness. On the other hand, teens with leukemia may experience real friendship.

When John was diagnosed with leukemia, **John, Age 17** he had to stop playing baseball. His baseball buddies soon drifted away, except for Doug. This surprised John. He had never been really close to Doug. Doug stuck in there, though. He visited John in the hospital. The two boys talked and watched TV. Sometimes Doug just sat quietly by John's bed. John felt better knowing he was not alone.

School

Doing well in school is important to most teens. They need to attend classes and get good grades in order to graduate. They need to have a good high school record to get into college. Leukemia can affect a teen's success in school. Frequent absences due to illness and treatment can make it difficult to meet graduation requirements.

Sandy is a high school junior with leukemia. Every month, she must miss

Sandy, Age 16

several days of school for treatment. Sandy and her parents meet with her teachers at the beginning of each semester. They explain Sandy's situation.

Sandy's teachers work out assignments for her. They guarantee that she can make up tests. The school has set aside attendance requirements for her. Sandy also participates in a tutoring program. The school's cooperation and Sandy's hard work enable her to keep up and do well.

Planning for the Future

Most teens make plans for the future. They might decide what college to attend or what job they want. They may look forward to someday having children. Leukemia can make the future a big question mark. Teens with leukemia may worry about getting well. They may fear a relapse. They wonder if they should bother to plan for the years ahead.

For every 100,000 high school students, 14 will be diagnosed with some form of cancer. Today's teens have a 6 percent greater chance of getting cancer than teens did 20 or 30 years ago. No one knows why. There is good news, however. Today's teens have a greater chance of surviving their cancer than teens in the past.

Fast Fact

While no one can predict the future, teens and children with leukemia can have hope. Childhood leukemia is one of the most treatable forms of cancer. More children and teens with acute lymphocytic leukemia are surviving than ever before. The overall five-year survival rate is now 80 percent. In 1960, the survival rate was only 4 percent.

Ways to Cope

Most teens are natural optimists. This attitude can help teens with leukemia battle their disease. If you are a teen with leukemia, here are suggestions for ways to cope:

Learn all you can about leukemia.
This is a way to feel in control. Take an active part in your treatment. Ask questions. Ask to be allowed to make decisions. For example, decide in which vein to start the IV or which injection you want first. Even small decisions will make you feel less helpless.

Keep a journal of your treatment.
Include the date and name and amount of medications. Note the side effects and how you felt. Share this information with your doctor. It will help the doctor plan your treatment.

Teens should conduct regular self-examinations for cancer. Girls can examine their breasts for lumps. Lumps might be a sign of breast cancer. Boys can examine their testicles.

Learn to manage stress.

Exercise, listen to music, read a book, or share your feelings with someone. Relaxation exercises or meditation may help. Stress and anxiety can keep you from getting better. Your health care team can guide you on ways to manage stress.

Attend meetings of a support group.

There are groups just for teens with cancer. You will get a lot of encouragement and emotional support. You will learn how other teens with cancer deal with their problems.

Try to maintain a normal schedule as much as possible.

This will help keep your mind off your illness. You will not feel so different. If you are in the hospital, you will be on the hospital's schedule. Even so, following a routine can help you keep things together.

Keep yourself well groomed.

You will feel better. If you are in the hospital, wear your own clothes. You will feel more like yourself.

Focus on something besides your leukemia.

Try a new hobby or activity. Meeting the challenge of something new will boost your self-esteem.

Be prepared to educate other people about your disease.
Even adults may not understand. Some people may even think
you're contagious. You can set them straight. Let other people
know how you want to be treated.

**Be ready with three or four suggestions when people ask what
they can do for you.**
They might fix your favorite food or get a certain book from the
library. Let people know you appreciate their help. They'll feel
good about helping. You might feel better knowing they feel
better!

Be open and honest about your feelings.
This is different from trying to be cheerful all the time. You need
to express anger, fear, and worry. Covering these feelings with
false cheer will only make you feel worse.

Points to Consider

How do you act around someone who is seriously ill? Why
do you have that reaction?

What could you do to help a teen with leukemia?

What ideas do you have for ways teens with leukemia might
cope with their illness?

Chapter Overview

Advances in leukemia research and treatment have improved the survival rate for people with leukemia.

Research continues along several avenues. These include gene therapy, biological therapy, bone marrow transplants, and drug therapy.

People with leukemia can participate in clinical trials. Clinical trials help doctors find out if a new treatment is safe and effective.

New forms of treatment promise to push the survival rate for leukemia even higher.

Chapter 7

Looking Ahead

A diagnosis of leukemia once was a death sentence. This is no longer true. Many more people with leukemia are living longer. They are living normal lives. Children and teens have an especially good chance of beating leukemia.

Since 1960, the chance for long-term remission or cure in children with leukemia has gone from 5 to 75 percent. The improved rate of survival reflects advances in the treatment of leukemia. These advances have come about through research. As research continues, the survival rates for all types of leukemia will climb even higher.

Cancer no longer has to be a scary word. At least half of all people diagnosed with cancer today will survive.

Avenues for Research

Leukemia research is following several main avenues. One avenue is gene therapy, or genetic engineering. Researchers hope to find out why normal genes turn into cancer genes. Then researchers might be able to keep this from happening. They might be able to identify people at risk for leukemia. Incorrect genes could be removed and replaced with correct genes. Gene therapy involves basic research into the causes of leukemia.

A second avenue of research is biological therapy. Researchers are looking for ways to stimulate the immune system to fight leukemia. Biological therapy is already being used to treat some forms of leukemia. It uses a substance called interferon. This substance helps the immune system slow the growth of abnormal white cells. Biological therapy also uses substances called interleukins. These substances encourage the growth of healthy white cells.

A third avenue of research involves ways to improve bone marrow transplants. Researchers hope to eliminate or reduce the need for heavy doses of chemotherapy before transplant. The drugs and radiation presently given are very hard on the people. Researchers also are looking for ways to prevent graft-versus-host disease. Most of all, they would like the ability to use donor marrow different from that of the person. This would make many more bone marrow transplants possible.

A fourth avenue of research is to find better drugs with fewer side effects. Drugs are needed that will kill leukemia cells and not normal cells. Drug research includes the best way to administer a drug. Researchers want to know if a drug is more effective when given by mouth or by injection. Drug research also includes monitoring the body's responses to drugs. Researchers want to know why resistance to a certain drug develops in some people. They want to pinpoint the exact moment the resistance begins. Then doctors can step in with another form of treatment.

Clinical Trials

People with leukemia can help advance knowledge about the disease. They can do this by participating in clinical trials. Clinical trials are studies to find out better ways to prevent, diagnose, or treat a disease. Many clinical trials involve testing new drugs or combinations of drugs. Clinical trials follow strict scientific procedures.

People need to think carefully before deciding to join a clinical trial. On the one hand, they may benefit from the new treatment. On the other hand, there are always risks involved in something experimental. Most of today's effective treatments resulted from clinical trials. A participant may not directly benefit. Even so, he or she might have the satisfaction of having helped others.

Researchers are working on a test that can detect tiny amounts of leukemia cells. The test is called polymerase chain reaction (PCR). With this test, relapses are easier to predict in people in remission. PCR detects traces of leukemia. These traces help doctors predict how likely a person will be to relapse. Doctors then could find and treat the leukemia sooner.

Mack has a rare form of leukemia. So far, his doctors have managed to control the disease. Mack wants to do more. He found a clinical trial related to his type of leukemia. He used the Physician Data Query (PDQ) on the Internet to locate the study. Mack was excited. The trial was being conducted at a medical center near his home.

Mack, Age 18

Mack showed the information to his doctors. They thought that he was eligible. They helped him enroll. Mack will not know for several months if the new treatment will help. In the meantime, he is glad to be doing something to fight leukemia.

Hope for the Future

The rate of cure for leukemia will continue to rise. People with leukemia can have hope for the future.

Julie is a high school junior and a leukemia survivor. She spent her early childhood

Julie, Age 17

battling acute lymphocytic leukemia. It has been in remission for seven years. Julie celebrates two birthdays every year. She celebrates the day she was born and the day the doctor told her she was cured. Julie still remembers the chemotherapy and the trips to the hospital. Now, however, she talks excitedly about her plans for the future.

Points to Consider

How could your school help raise money for leukemia research?

Would you participate in a clinical trial? Why or why not?

What can you do to educate other people about leukemia?

Glossary

acute (uh-KYOOT)—appearing suddenly, increasing rapidly, and getting worse quickly

anemia (uh-NEE-mee-uh)—a low number of red blood cells; a person with anemia may look pale and feel tired and weak.

aspiration (ass-pur-AY-shuhn)—withdrawing fluid or tissue from the body, especially by means of suction

biopsy (BYE-op-see)—removal and examination of fluid and tissue from the living body; doctors perform biopsies to aid in diagnoses.

chronic (KRON-ik)—lasting for a long time

contagious (kuhn-TAY-juhss)—capable of being spread from person to person

immune system (i-MYOON SISS-tuhm)—the system that protects the body from illness and disease

interferon (in-tur-FIHR-on)—a chemical used in biological therapy; interferon helps the immune system slow the rate of growth and division of cancer cells.

interleukin (in-tur-LOO-kin)—a substance used in biological therapy; an interleukin encourages the growth and activities of certain kinds of white blood cells.

nausea (NAW-zee-uh)—upset stomach

oncologist (ahn-KAH-luh-jist)—a doctor who specializes in diagnosing and treating cancer

radiation (ray-dee-AY-shuhn)—energy that spreads out from a source such as radium

relapse (REE-laps)—the return of symptoms after a period of improvement

remission (ri-MISH-uhn)—a period when there are no active signs of a disease or illness

resistance (ri-ZISS-tuhnss)—being opposed to or against something; withstanding something.

For More Information

Gold, John C., and Thomas Keating. *Cancer.* Parsippany, NJ: Crestwood House, 1997.

Huegel, Kelly. *Young People and Chronic Illness.* Minneapolis: Free Spirit, 1998.

Landau, Elaine. *Cancer.* New York: Twenty-First Century Books, 1995.

Siegel, Dorothy Schainman, and David E. Newton. *Leukemia.* New York: Franklin Watts, 1994.

Useful Addresses and Internet Sites

American Cancer Society
1599 Clifton Road NE
Atlanta, GA 30329
1-800-ACS-2345

Canadian Cancer Society
10 Alcorn Avenue
Suite 200
Toronto, ON M4V 3B1
CANADA

Candlelighters Childhood Cancer Foundation
7910 Woodmont Avenue
Suite 460
Bethesda, MD 20814
1-800-366-2223

Leukemia Society of America
600 Third Avenue
New York, NY 10016
1-800-955-4LSA

American Cancer Society
http://www.cancer.org
Provides general and detailed information
on cancer

Candlelighters Childhood Cancer Foundation
http://www.candlelighters.org
Educates and supports children with cancer,
their families, and their caregivers

Leukemia Society of America
http://www.leukemia.org
Dedicated to curing leukemia and improving
life for patients and their families

National Cancer Institute
http://www.nci.nih.gov
Supports research and provides information
about cancer

Index

acute leukemia, 13, 14, 19, 21. *See also* lymphocytic leukemia; myelogenous leukemia
anemic, 7
appearance, 47, 52

benzene, 10
biological therapy, 56
birth defects, 10
bleeding without clotting, 7, 21, 34
blood, 6–7, 21, 35
    tests, 23, 28, 29
body image, 47
bone marrow, 7, 23–24, 32
    tests, 23–24, 28, 29
    transplant, 31–33, 56
bruising easily, 7, 20, 21

Camp Baldy, 42
Cancer Information Service (CIS), 41
cancer,
    learning from other patients, 42, 52
    survivors, 43
    types, 6
    warning signs of, 22
catheter, 29
chemicals, 10
chemical tests, 23
chemotherapy, 28–30, 43, 47, 48, 59
    side effects, 29, 30
Chernobyl Nuclear Power Plant, 9
chronic leukemia, 14, 15, 20, 21. *See also* lymphocytic leukemia; myelogenous leukemia

clinical trials, 57, 58
communication. *See* talking
counselors, 39, 40, 41, 42, 48

death, 6, 55
donors, 7, 32, 33, 35
Down syndrome, 10
drug research, 57
drug therapy. *See* chemotherapy

education, 51, 53
emotional support, 38, 42, 44, 52
emotions, 5, 6, 24–25, 38, 39, 40, 48, 53

First Connection, 40
friends, 29, 44, 49
future, 50–51, 58–59

genes, 9
gene therapy, 56
genetic disorders, 10
government services, 41
graft-versus-host disease, 32, 56
granulocytes, 15

hair loss, 29, 30, 31, 47
health care providers, 38–39

immunity, 8
independence, 48
infections, 8, 21, 34, 49
interferon, 56
interleukins, 56
Internet, 43, 58